THE RISE AND FALL
OF KING SAUL

K. LEE

AuthorKLee.com

KLEPub.com

THE RISE AND FALL OF KING SAUL

Published by Krystal Lee Enterprises (KLE Publishing) Copyright © 2022 by K. Lee All rights reserved. Please send comments and questions:
Krystal Lee Enterprises
770-240-0089 Ext. 1
sales@KLEPub.com
To Reach the Author:
Email: info@authorklee.com
Web: AuthorKLee.com
Social Media: @AuthorKLee

Printed in the United States of America.
All rights reserved. No part of this book may be reproduced or transmitted in any form or by any means, electronic or mechanical, including photocopying, recording or any information storage and retrieval system without written permission of the publisher except for brief quotations used in reviews, written specifically for inclusion in a newspaper, blog, magazine, or academic paper.

ISBN: 978-1-945066-34-4

Dedication

To my Lord and Savior, thank you for loving and saving me. Thank you for my children and their special place in my life. I have to thank my best friend and my mother, Yulanda Lucas. I love you to the moon and back. Grandaddy Lucas, you are a special jewel and a constant help.

To my siblings and those who are like family to me, I love you. I also want to thank my friends for reminding me to pursue my dreams. Apostle James Fowler, Bishop Steven L. Thompson, Dr. W. Michael Turner, and Bishop Wiliam Martin, thank you from my heart.

Of course, to you, the reader, may you be blessed by reading this book, and may the Good Lord be glorified.

Table of Contents

THE RISE of SAUL   7

HIS CHARACTER: HUMILITY   9

NATURAL GIFTS: LEADERSHIP 17

HIS ANOINTING: THE PRESENCE OF GOD   25

THE FALL of SAUL   35

DISOBEDIENCE: THE SHIFT   37

THE BELOVED IS REJECTED: A GRAVE ERROR 47

THE AFTERMATH: WHEN GOD'S PRESENCE LEAVES   59

A LESSON FOR US ALL   69

ABOUT THE AUTHOR 74

THE RISE of SAUL

His Character: Humility

1 Samuel 9: 3 NIV

3 Now the donkeys belonging to Saul's father Kish were lost, and Kish said to his son Saul, "Take one of the servants with you and go and look for the donkeys."

Many of us have humble beginnings; Christ even had a humble start, and Saul was no different. Saul was from the tribe of Benjamin, which was the smallest, youngest, and most humble tribe (1 Samuel 19:12-13). In life, we must remain humble and take our lessons with patience. The request Saul's father made of him to go out and track down the donkeys may not appear to be the mission of the century. In fact, the mission could have been successful or failed. Going on the search for the missing donkeys was a test of Saul's humility and a demonstration of his character.

Have you been asked to do something you felt at the time made no sense? I know as children, we are asked to clean everything, cook, wash walls, and take our siblings everywhere. It is tempting to think of yourself as a slave by how you are given tasks. At church, you may start in a humble position as well, cleaning bathrooms, serving food, volunteering to do whatever.

What do we learn from doing these seemingly minuscule tasks? What can a CEO learn from being a person at the bottom? I believe you get the building blocks for a strong foundation. I think it does add to what you understand about the entire business at hand. You also know what it means to start from an entry-level position to better relate to others and to find solutions at the top.

King Saul was no different. He had to pay his dues, and that started with searching for donkeys. Of all the animals to be sent out to recover, the Lord had Saul's dad send him out for donkeys. What do donkeys represent? What was their function—purpose, or importance for Saul and his family? Donkeys are creatures that are referenced several times in the Bible. The animal can bear very strong burdens and is considered a reliable helper to man.

This animal is also a symbol of peace, industry, and wealth. Donkeys are the beast chosen by God to demonstrate humility, trust, and mark epic moments in life. When Abraham used a donkey in Genesis 22:3 to help him and Isaac travel to where he was supposed to sacrifice his son.

"Abraham got up early in the morning to saddle his donkey, a small act, yet one of obedience to the Lord in order to offer Isaac up to God."

The text would have read very differently by intent and purpose if Abraham hadn't loaded up a donkey but a horse to go and sacrifice his son. Abraham also didn't pack a bag that he carried on his shoulders, but he saddled his donkey. A donkey helps men bear heavy burdens and is their helper in a time of need. We learn that Abraham was obedient to the Lord's command, and although his heart may have been heavy for the task, he also didn't waiver to be faithful.

Has the Lord asked you to do something that makes you feel heavy? That challenges you to think, is this God or the devil giving me this assignment? How many of us would have assumed it was a bad spirit that would tell us to kill our son? Murder is a sin, and this sin was also listed in the Ten Commandments given to Moses. Surely, God wouldn't want me to kill an innocent man to prove my love for Him, would He?

He didn't require the life of Isaac, but He was testing the faithfulness of Abraham. Sometimes Yah gives us commands to see if we will follow the instructions. The reason may come and sometimes even if it did, we still don't understand it. Sometimes it is simply because He said so. Why do we expect God to give us an account of why He makes certain requests? He is God of the Universe of everything living and dead, real or spirit.

We would be foolish not to trust God, and Abraham was no fool. He trusted the Lord and obeyed His request and he found the Lord to be faithful. Not only in saving his son's life but by giving him a son to begin with; he and his wife were old when they had Isaac.

In Numbers 22:23-35 the Spirit of God fell on the second animal ever to speak to man, and that animal was a donkey. He enabled the donkey to speak. The donkey did not open his mouth to curse the man, insult him, or fight him. This animal is not a warring animal but a helper even when he is being wronged.

The donkey saw the angel of the Lord standing in the path with a sword drawn when Balaam didn't. He was sticking his neck out to save the man by redirecting him. Similarly, Christ seeks to save us by redirecting our path from the crooked way to the straight. Balaam, however, was unaware of the animal's desire to help him, so he beat the animal three times for disobeying him. After the third beating, the Lord gave the caring beast speech.

The donkey said to Balaam. "Am I not your own donkey, which you have always ridden, to this day? Have I been in the habit of doing this to you?" "No," he said.

The donkey asked a question to Balaam and this question demonstrated his desire to still help him. When Balaam's eyes were opened, and he saw the angel with the sword, he knew then he had sinned. The donkey wasn't a stumbling block for the man but now a friend. Had the donkey not spoken and stopped him in his tracks, the angel said it would have slain Balaam because he was on a reckless path (Numbers 22:32-33).

Another account, and perhaps one of the most profound, was that the Lord Jesus "Yahshua" the Christ also rode on a donkey. Why not a horse? A horse symbolizes war, vengeance, and power, and it surely looks more kingly than a measly donkey. So why a donkey?

He was on a donkey because He had not come here to make war–yet. He came on a special assignment from His Father on High. The donkey symbolizes peace, being a help, a friend, and one who bears strong or heavy burdens for others. Yahshua rode through the crowd on a donkey because He was sent to help us.

He was sent to restore peace and communion between man and Yah. Jesus bore a load no other could bear so that man could be restored to the Father, the Creator of All. Yahshua will be coming at the second coming, riding on a horse. This horse does not represent peace, help, but war, judgment, vengeance, and vindication.

What else did we learn about the character of Saul? We learned he was committed to a task that demonstrated patience. Patience is a virtuous characteristic and if you have ever prayed for patience you will quickly find that the Lord provides you with a test that works patience. Patience comes when you realize your ability to move forward or change course is not within your control. Children are a true way to learn patience.

We learn patience and are not given it. This relationship reminds me also of how Christ left His home to put down his power to come here, be beneath angels, to comfort us. To be our help, guide, teacher, master, friend, and our everything. A loving parent does everything for a baby and they learn to love over time. Good thing God knew us before we were born. He had loved us before we were born.

Children can be stiff-necked and hard to budge, perhaps similar to goats. A baby goat is formerly known as a kid, and this is another adaptation we have made to address children. Maybe society did this because children can be just as headstrong as a goat!

One of the greatest tools for teaching children patience is repetition and corrective behaviors. The same way we learn to be patient with children is a similar example of how the Lord is also patient with us. God is the Father of His people, His children.

Have you learned that patience builds character and patience is the tree that gives the fruit of humility? The Lord says we ought to be like children (Matthew 18:3) so that we may enter into the Kingdom of God. That simply means we must be teachable; to mean we must be willing to listen and obey God the Father. The reason why we are commanded by God to obey our mother and father as children is because that same reverence we have for our natural father/mother, which we use towards Him when we are older.

If you never learn to fear your mother and father or reverence them, how can you know how to respect God? For that matter, how can we know how to treat others like teachers, elders, police officers, etc? If we don't learn to obey our mother and father, we are not trained to give any respect to someone else. Unruly children walk and run down a reckless path similar to Balaam, and those who choose that path just may find an Angel swinging a sword before them.

Thank the good Lord for the voices that are like the donkey in our lives that warn us to change direction, and not to cross in front of a swinging sword to our peril. Many youths are passing away and dropping like flies because they are living reckless lives and not heading in the direction of the Teacher. The ultimate teacher is the Lord and we must take him seriously—respect Him because He is mighty and Holy.

We shouldn't live recklessly because no man knows the hour when Christ will return or when grace will run out. You don't want to look up and notice that the Spirit of God is gone, and you are walking alone. Remember, no matter where you go in life, stay humble and continue to listen to God because His children never outgrow their Master.

Luke 6:40 says, "We are never above our teacher but are fully trained to be like our teacher." As believers, we are to look like our Father. We are to look like Yahshua (Jesus) without trying to replace His presence or Lordship in our lives. Saul later stopped governing himself according to God's word with an unreproachable heart of gratitude. He no longer had this child-like faith but attempted to be equal with God. He forgot to reverence the Lord as Holy and wiser than himself, but we will talk more about that in "The Fall of Saul."

NATURAL GIFTS: LEADERSHIP

1 Samuel 9: 15-17 NIV

15 Now the day before Saul came, the Lord had revealed this to Samuel:

16 "About this time tomorrow I will send you a man from the land of Benjamin. Anoint him ruler over my people Israel; he will deliver them from the hand of the Philistines. I have looked on my people, for their cry has reached me."

17 When Samuel caught sight of Saul, the Lord said to him, "This is the man I spoke to you about; he will govern my people."

Do you know how important it is for us to be able to hear the Voice of Yah? Is it a voice in your ear, a scripture you turn to in your Bible, or an inner knowing that has no clear voice but delivers instructions? No matter your connection, be sure to hear from God to be certain of your journey.

Many ask the question, is God pleased with me? The truth is if you are in His will, even if you please no one else, you will be pleasing God. Your obedience and devotion are what He wants. Samuel was devoted to Yah even as a child. He was a first fruit gift from his mother, Hannah to Yah.

When Samuel received instructions from the Almighty to prepare for a king, He would pick from the tribe of Benjamin; he knew his assignment. God was also specific with His instructions. For God, time is not of the essence. He is the author of time, and no clock dictates His plans but His sovereignty.

Time is more beneficial for man in communicating because we are not omnipresent or omniscient. We need a way to track and keep up with each other, and time helps us to do that. Can you imagine setting a meeting or making plans without a way to track time? The answer should be "no" because the chances of the meeting happening are slim if you both are not on the same metric for gauging time.

Our number one goal should be to have the same timezone as God. Hence, His will, plans, and vision for our lives should take precedence over anything else. This might not sound great in the beginning because we all, at one point, thought we knew enough to determine what direction we would take, only to find that we were wrong and Yah had the right answer all along.

The right next step requires us to get in step with God. To get into step, we must see the value in His way and choose that over our own. We are to seek the Kingdom of God and His righteousness so that all things will be added unto us (Matthew 6:33).

Another truth we must accept is God's timing doesn't consult us for our opinion or approval. God speaks and what He says is final, perfect, true, and must not be changed. The Lord requires our obedience to His command because the Bible reads, "You are not a true believer unless you follow His commandments (John 14:15)." In addition, He says obedience is better than sacrifice, and His sheep know His voice (John 10:27).

The Lord gives us all gifts because we are His children, and He prepares us to serve in His kingdom. Spiritual gifts are a heavily visited topic among believers because gifts feed the body. Gifts were given to build up the saints of God, and collectively, we are to operate like one body to help lead the unbeliever to Christ. Without understanding your gifts, you cannot know your function in God or be certain you will fulfill your purpose. Your purpose and gifts are connected, and they work together.

Although there are tools many use often, like quizzes, tests, and others, to determine their gifts in 20 to 100 questions, the best method is using the Bible. Who best to tell you your gifts than

God? He knows why He made you, and although you may not have the appearance of your assignment at the moment, Yah will take you the rest of the way. There is no caste system in God, where you are born of a preacher, so you are called to become one. His kingdom is not made out of man's traditions but His choosing.

Now, the risk we take when we leave God out of the process of searching for our purpose and gifts is that we may be malfunctioning in the body. Can you imagine seeing a body haphazardly put together like Frankenstein? The hands are where the feet should be. The arms are legs, the head is spun in the wrong direction, and the list goes on and on. What can the body accomplish if people are not in the right position to be the hands and feet of God? The body functions as a plague or cancerous cell if we are not operating to represent the kingdom God is building here on earth.

First, in 1 Corinthians 12, we learn that gifts from the Lord include wisdom, knowledge, faith, healing, miracles, prophecy, distinguishing between spirits (discernment), tongues, and the interpretation of tongues (1 Corinthians 12:7-10). All these are empowered by the Spirit of God, who apportions to each individually as He wills (1 Corinthians 12:11). The Lord has a plan for your life, and your gift is an asset for getting you in right position to win.

In Ephesians 4:11, the spiritual gifts that make-up what is commonly called the "five-fold ministry" is given. The "five-fold ministry" comprises apostles, prophets, evangelists, preachers, and teachers. These gifts are bestowed upon God's children for the edification of the body of Christ. Gifts are not given for man to decide how to be used but for the Lord's instruction.

Let's briefly revisit the parable explaining spiritual gifts (Matthew 25:14-30). God gave three people gifts, which were reflected in talents or shekels. The three varied in what they did with their talents. The two that did the will of the Lord and returned a harvest used their talent for the edification of the Kingdom, and they got a greater reward. The foolish man, who buried the talent and returned nothing on top of what he was given, was called a lazy, wicked servant and cast out the gates.

Choosing to use your talent for God and not bury the gifts He has given you, then trusting Him for instruction is the ideal posture. In the case of Saul, instruction was very much needed as he didn't appear to be qualified to be the King of the Hebrew nation; in fact, no man is qualified without God to lead even themselves. For him to have a fighting chance to lead them, he had to seek the Lord every step of the way because there was no king before him. There was something about Saul that the Lord liked that made Him choose Saul to become king.

One of Saul's gifts was leadership, and his two other gifts were wisdom and knowledge. These gifts were birthed in him long before he realized but they needed to be cultivated. The first lesson any good leader ought to learn or possess is a teachable spirit. Before anyone can lead, they must first know how to follow. Saul had to hear the voice of the Lord and follow the commands of God because he had to lay the foundation for God's people.

Saul had already proved in his youth that he was capable and raised to listen and follow the voice of his father. The foundation was there for him to listen to his heavenly Father's Voice also. If we don't pass the first step, we will likely be impeded in our ability to follow the next step. Saul's next step was to learn the path of God and, after learning it, to lead by example. He had to spend lots of time with God and God's appointed people to develop and mature the talents God put in him. Developing your gifts allows for the Lord to call on you to serve.

Can you imagine a young man growing up in our society, void of the foundation to obey his parents, ever making a true attempt to follow the rules? These children are picked out by the time they are in 3rd grade to support the system. The system writes off children who cannot follow the rules as the future of the prison industrial complex.

When in band or sports camps, you must learn routines and be active during practice. If you are not active in practice, the coach will not see what you can do, so he will not put you in the game. Practice must be taken just as seriously as the real game. Same as if you were a singer or an artist. You don't hold back for the real thing.

When you study the Word of God, seek to learn with purpose because lives depend on it. As you learn, you will be put through tests and given chances to live out what you learn. As Saul trained, he was given more tests and room to make decisions and keep himself on God's team. The donkey mission was practice for his calling to be king of the Hebrews.

In verse 15, we see another gift at work: prophecy. Samuel was called as a young man to serve the Lord, but before he became the prophet we know, he did tasks like sweeping the floors, I am sure doing the dishes and serving Ely by doing other tasks about the church. Even when God first called his name, and he answered, he was not ready to be fully used by God because he wasn't mature in his gifting yet. However, as he grew in the Lord, he was trusted to serve Him.

Committing to developing your gifts is vital to being in God's will. Following God, we must decrease so that He can increase within us. Samuel and Saul were stewards for the owner; the owner is the Lord God Almighty, and the earth belongs to Him. We are all required to function in the body as His Spirit works overall and through all and in all (Ephesians 4:6).

Saul did not tell God to choose him, in fact, he tried to talk Samuel and God out of it. He had more excuses for why he shouldn't be king than to be king. Have you ever tried to talk yourself out of things God intended for you? If you choose to be putty in His hands, he can use you.

God saw this virtue in Saul when He chose him. God chooses us, and if we want Him to draw near to us, we must first draw near to Him (James 4:8). We get close so that we may hear what thus says the Lord. Something of note is that when God gives us gifts, He anoints them so we can serve.

HIS ANOINTING: AND THE PRESENCE OF GOD

Saul had no possible way of growing to be king in the natural. He was from the youngest tribe, with the lowest hierarchy and the smallest in number. All the way around, he would appear to be the wrong candidate for the job.

If there were a vote by the people, he would have also failed because his money was not long enough to win a campaign. The King's anointing that God gave him put him in a position he could never have earned. Yes, the presence of the Lord, His anointing married to our gift(s), will make the impossible possible.

I Samuel 14: 47 – 48

47 After Saul had assumed rule over Israel, he fought against their enemies on every side: Moab, the Ammonites, Edom, the kings of Zobah, and the Philistines. Wherever he turned, he inflicted punishment on them.

48 He fought valiantly and defeated the Amalekites, delivering Israel from the hands of those who had plundered them.

In Deuteronomy 28:9-11 the Bible reads, "We are blessed in the city and blessed in the field;" furthermore, He says He will make us "prosper" and "abound" in everything we do. This same truth is supported by 1 Samuel 14:47-48 when the Bible states having the Presence of God as you carry out divine assignments results in victory. When we walk with the Spirit of God, it is equivalent to walking with the Ark of the Covenant. The presence of God has to be with you at all times for the victory to be yours and for Him to fight your battles. When the Lord fights your battles, it may not make sense or look achievable to the natural eyes, but the spiritual eyes see you winning.

Saul was able to defeat the Moabites, Ammonites, Edomites, etc. not because he was the King of Israel, but because the Presence of God was with him. A grave mistake Saul would later make was to believe the power and influence he had was his own. His influence was borrowed. Like how Deuteronomy 28 listed blessings in obedience, it also listed curses for those that didn't do what the Lord said.

Don't let adversity fool you into believing that the Presence of God is not in your life. During our battles, the Lord can be glorified because He makes us triumphant over our problems, situations, and our enemies. Challenges will come to us all. Saul had battle after battle that he had to fight, and God gave him the victory.

That same God can give you victory in any facet of your life, and surely, where He commanded you to go, He is able to pave the way. Keep the Presence of God in your life and conform your lifestyle to a victorious one. Where the Spirit of the Lord is, our battles will always be won, and the favor of the Lord will be on our lives.

I Samuel 10: 7

7 Once these signs are fulfilled, do whatever your hand finds to do, for God is with you.

If you have been gifted with a gift from the Lord, there are requirements and responsibilities assigned to you to operate your gift according to Godly standards. In the case of Saul, he was anointed for two things. He had a kingly anointing and a prophetic one (1 Samuel 10-6-7, 10-13).

Saul was able to communicate with God directly, and this had to be a requirement, as another man had never had this post of King over the Hebrews. God personalized his quest for Saul and spoke with him directly. He was active in governing Israel and gave Saul access to His divine throne room by way of the prophetic.

This gift was not bestowed on every king.

Many men were kings in the Bible and they all did not have access to the throne room of God. I believe Yah gifted Saul with the ability to have access to Him so that He could stay encouraged and not faint or doubt. When you hear the Voice of the Lord, you have peace, and there is nothing you fear.

Saul, coming from an inferior background, stepping up in a major way to lead warriors in battle, and take a throne without a printed book was a large undertaken. With the Presence of God and the Voice of God in his ear, He had to feel confident in Yah's ability to deliver Israel no matter the circumstance. In addition, God gifted him with the prophetic so that the manifestation of total obedience would continuously come forth throughout his reign. "For I know My sheep, My sheep know Me, and they hear My voice (John 10:27).

I Samuel 15:3

3 Now go, attack the Amalekites and totally destroy all that belongs to them. Do not spare them; put to death men and women, children and infants, cattle and sheep, camels and donkeys."

Saul was very acquainted with the Presence of God and saw the manifestation of signs and wonders. His prophetic gifting appeared in less than 24 hours after Samuel prophesied it. He was seen doing miracle after miracle, including his ability to speak in the prophetic.

Saul was following the Voice of the Lord and reaping the benefits from his obedience and trust in Him. Your obedience to God guarantees the stability of the Presence of God in your life. Saul learned this and mastered it, but did he keep it at heart?

In our lives, we can reach a low point. We can experience a life-altering situation where we are the victim, and by God's grace, He delivers us, and we become the victor. When you have victory after victory, some may lose sight of why they are victorious. When we displace God and attempt to rob Him of His glory, we are out of His will. When we are out of His will, we can forfeit our blessings.

Have you ever felt the frustration of encountering ungrateful children? Since birth, children were cared for, provided for, fed by, and loved by their parents. When the child grew up, they went to college, graduated, and then got a great job in part because of their parents. Then, all of a sudden, they are too busy for their parents. They no longer care about their parents' quality of life.

The prodigal son is the prime example of how some children who are raised well encounter what appears to be a blessing: money, and when they get it, they lose their minds. Something happens to man when we encounter wealth, riches, and power: If we have not girded our flesh and weighed it down with the Word, our flesh will attempt to overthrow the Spirit. Sometimes, this is a subtle change in thinking, actions, or belief that leads to a world of regret and sin.

In 1 Samuel 15:3, The Lord told him to go (command) and attack the Amalekites. Kill the king, kill all the people, and destroy everything that they had. When the Lord gives a command, it is imperative for you, us, to listen because sometimes there are no redos. The prophet didn't get a redo; he was mauled by the lion and died for disobedience (1 Samuel 17:36). Ananias and Sapphira were struck dead for not giving the church what they committed—no redo (Acts 5:1-11). Achan in Joshua was told to take nothing, but he took coins and a coat for his wife, which cost him his life and the lives of his entire family—no redo (Joshua 7:21).

In your Christian walk with Christ, do you always remain sensitive to the voice of God? In the situation of a divine command, we must obey or run the risk of removing the presence and protection of God from our lives. Sometimes in life, we are tempted to disobey an order from God, and disobedience has consequences. The enemy waits to entrap us with the spirit of compromise. An account that demonstrates the importance of obedience is the story of Iddo. Iddo was the name of the prophet killed by a lion because he disobeyed a direct order from God.

This prophet was a mighty man of Yah. He had a personal relationship with God where the Lord gave him instructions and expected him to follow them (1 Kings 13:1-10). The prophet did well in bringing the message to the king and obeying God's decree to take nothing in exchange. He was supposed to hurry home after giving the message and not spend the night.

This prophet did as he was requested by the king. He went to the king, gave him a message, and prayed with him for his hand to be restored, and it was. The king offered him gifts, food, and lodging, which he declined. He then set out to go home as the Lord commanded.

On his way home, an old prophet came to him and told him he had a message from God for him. He told the prophet that the Lord told him he ought to eat and drink with him back at his house. The prophet decided to go back and eat and drink in the land the Lord told him not to spend the night.

He disobeyed the Lord's order. When Iddo left for home the next day, he found that his disobedience would cost him his life! The presence of God covered Iddo when he was in His will. To deny a king was a grave insult, but the Lord's presence kept him safe.

When he disobeyed the Lord's command and went back to eat and drink with another prophet, the protection from the Lord was removed from His servant. A lion killed him when he was on his journey home, but his body was not devoured (1 Kings 13:26). The lion was not feasting on him because of hunger, but the lion was on assignment by God. The animals reverence God's authority on the earth.

What else did the prophet find next to Iddo? The old prophet told his sons to saddle his donkey as he departed for the body. When the prophet arrived at Iddo's body, the lion and a donkey were standing near each other. The lion did not kill the donkey that looked onward at his master, nor did it eat the remains from Iddo. It was on the back of the donkey that the old prophet brought the body of Iddo to town for a proper burial.

We must remember our humble beginnings. The same relationship you start with God, keep that relationship close to your mind, heart, ears, hands, and soul (will and emotions). Iddo wasn't a bad prophet; he was faithful to what God told him to do until he listened to someone else he thought knew more than he did. We have to be careful who we listen to because not everyone who gets us off track appears as an enemy. Who knows if God told the old prophet to test Iddo or if the prophet was mistaken about the voice he heard? The issue is that Iddo was certain of his instructions, and those were the ones he was punished for breaking.

To know to do good and do it not is sin (James 4:17). Sin, when it is full-grown, leads to death (James 1:15). Never forget to remain like a child in the presence of God and take every Word from His mouth seriously. Your obedience or lack thereof could cost you to sin unto death (1 John 5:16).

Somehow, Saul would lose his way as a child of God, which is a requirement to keep the Presence of God in your life. It should bring great comfort to know that we don't have to be strong warriors or the best at anything for the Lord to bless us. He says to us that in our weakness, He is made strong, so take courage if you don't feel you are the best or you lack the resources to excel; that will not stop the plans God has for you (2 Corinthians 12:9- 10)!

Iddo had a promising future to be used like

Samuel, but he couldn't compromise. What would make the life and tragic end of Iddo align with the life of Saul? What went wrong? How did Saul, who was so close to Yah, slip into disobedience, compromise, and lose the Presence of God? In the Fall of Saul, we will see how that happened. Let our study continue to 1 Samuel 9:15-17.

The Fall of Saul

DISOBEDIENCE: THE SHIFT

I Samuel 15: 7 – 9

7 Then Saul attacked the Amalekites all the way from Havilah to Shur, near the eastern border of Egypt.

8 He took Agag king of the Amalekites alive, and all his people he totally destroyed with the sword.

9 But Saul and the army spared Agag and the best of the sheep and cattle, the fat calves and lambs—everything that was good. These they were unwilling to destroy completely, but everything that was despised and weak they totally destroyed.

Saul did what was tempting to any man to do: to try and interpret what God meant instead of listening to what He said. Don't try to rationalize the Word God gave to benefit your liking. Don't try to bend His command to fit your lifestyle, desire, ministry platform, or anything else.

A lie is when you bend the truth even a little bit. The Bible instructs us not to add nor take away from the Word (Revelation 22:18-20). When we change and alter God's Word to fit our liking, we have accepted another gospel and it is as Paul asks, "Who has bewitched you (Galatians 3:1)?" Saul was jumped or succumbed to the spirit of iniquity. Iniquity is a premeditated choice and continuance of sin without repentance (GotQuestions.org).

The Lord specifically told him to destroy everything that the Amalekites had in their possession and take nothing. King Saul, however, didn't follow those instructions. He destroyed some of their things killed most of the people, but took the glamorous and glittering things. The healthy animals he kept, and he spared the life of the king.

Now, what was going on in Saul's mind? What seduced him to believe that "A," God would be okay with him changing His plans? "B," that there would be no consequence for his disobedience—or that he could bear the punishment?

The trick of the enemy is to have your eyes set in one place while he plots to have you fail. King Saul wasn't tricked neither was Eve wasn't either in the garden. They both willfully chose to disobey God under the guise they knew better. They thought their supposed good intentions would outweigh their consequence. Sometimes, aren't we capable of thinking the end justifies the means?

Disobedience is not an uncommon practice. All of us, because we are all tempted to disobey Him, distance ourselves when we embrace a lie over truth. In hindsight, we can all point to decisions we grew to regret. I don't think we can thank the Lord enough for his mercy and goodness because He allows us to repent and turn back. Some of us, however, don't have enough time or the ability to turn back after being given over to a reprobate mind (Romans 1:28). Nebuchadnezzar was a man who doubted God, and He allowed him—the king to lose his mind. It wasn't until the Lord permitted him to come to himself that he was restored from his beastly appearance, which took several years (Daniel 4:32-33).

A question I want to ask Saul, and really any of us when we disobey God, is, why? There was something Saul must have wanted that went outside of God's desire for him. Something caught his eye, attention, and changed his direction. The first thing that makes many of us sinful is being materialistic.

I Samuel 15: 13 – 15

13 When Samuel reached him, Saul said, "The Lord bless you! I have carried out the Lord's instructions."

14 But Samuel said, "What then is this bleating of sheep in my ears? What is this lowing of cattle that I hear?"

15 Saul answered, "The soldiers brought them from the Amalekites; they spared the best of the sheep and cattle to sacrifice to the Lord your God, but we totally destroyed the rest."

Saul took God's Voice for granted and assumed disobeying God wouldn't be a big deal. I don't think he believed he wouldn't get caught, but then again, his playing the blame game could imply that theory. I am not sure what made Saul believe he could conceal the truth from God. He bought into a very nasty lie, and to support the lie, he needed more misgivings to support his decision.

Saul deviated from the command of God because he rested on his thinking and understanding. The Bible tells us not to lean on our own understanding but to rely on every Word from God (Proverbs 3:5-6). Saul is left without excuse because he could hear and knew the Voice of the Lord. He had the presence of God operating in his life to an undeniable degree, and yet he thought he could lie and hide like Adam and Eve when he also sinned.

We will not be able to sweet talk God, conceal our true heart's desire or intent, or defend our actions with lies. God is omnipresent, omnipotent, and knows all His children intimately (Jeremiah 1:5). Anytime we deviate or disobey God's command, it gets more difficult for that person to come back to God if they don't stop at the first sight of sin. All sins can be forgiven except blaspheming against the Holy Spirit. (Mark 3:28-30). Saul was supposed to go and report to Samuel after the battle, but he didn't come. Samuel had to go and confront Saul.

When Samuel confronted Saul, he didn't own his mistake but tried to hide it. When Samuel told Saul he knew he was lying, then Saul confessed he kept the items for God. How can he think sinning against God and keeping items He already said He didn't want would bless Him? The short, he lied. Fresh and salt water cannot come out of the same vessel, nor can disobedience be supported by the notion "I sinned to please God;" it is an oxymoron (James 3:11).

I believe the prophet Samuel was there not only to rebuke King Saul for his disobedience to the Lord but also to extend an opportunity for him to get in right step with God. Saul was given a chance to admit, fess up, and repent for his actions, but instead, he blamed others after being found out. When the Lord was walking in the garden in the cool of the day, He approached Adam and Eve, and the two of them were dressed in fig leaves because the serpent told them they were naked (Genesis 3:8-13).

When God questioned them further, Adam blamed Eve for disobeying God's command. Why do we think there is a scapegoat when we sin? This did not stop God's judgment of Saul. The best thing to do when we sin is to own our decision, repent, and turn away from the wicked way. I don't think Saul truly realized that knowing God intimately was a gift. God desired to forgive Saul, but his selfishness kept the two divided because God had nothing to do with sin (Isaiah 59:2-3).

I Samuel 15: 17 – 19

17 Samuel said, "Although you were once small in your own eyes, did you not become the head of the tribes of Israel? The Lord anointed you king over Israel.

18 And he sent you on a mission, saying, 'Go and completely destroy those wicked people, the Amalekites; wage war against them until you have wiped them out.'

19 Why did you not obey the Lord? Why did you pounce on the plunder and do evil in the eyes of the Lord?"

After King Saul did not own his sin and repent, his allegiance to God shifted from doing the work of the Lord to doing and justifying his own plans. He was no longer concerned about how his sin hurt God nor concerned about how his sin would affect him. He got away from his first love and began the transition of allegiance from God to satan. He couldn't repent because he didn't agree that he was in error. He blamed others for his choices during the invasion, but he could have changed their actions as Joshua corrected violations in the past.

He was the leader of the tribes of Israel. He was the one anointed and put in charge of ruling the people, so he was responsible for the fall. As the King of Israel, he got the praise and the correction for when the people errored. Therefore, it was his final call to make the people get in right step with God, but he didn't choose to do that. If this was not Saul's idea in the inception, it became his choice because he sided with the voice of men over the command of God.

To determine your allegiance, you have to look at what governs your decision-making. Do you align and profess the truth of the Bible or societal norms? Do you agree with God or man when it comes to serious and trivial matters? Do you meditate, study the Word, or spend time with God? If your thoughts, opinions, or the opinions of people in the world are held in higher importance than God's positions on a matter, your allegiance is not with God.

We are not called to question God's authority; we are allowed, however, to ask Him questions. God permits us to come boldly to the throne of grace (Hebrews 4:16). We serve a mighty and powerful God who is the King of all Kings, and He sets all men in position for the judgment or benefit of nations. Nothing in life happens without his knowledge (Lamentations 3:37).

I Samuel 15: 20 – 22

20 "But I did obey the Lord," Saul said. "I went on the mission the Lord assigned me. I completely destroyed the Amalekites and brought back Agag their king.

21 The soldiers took sheep and cattle from the plunder, the best of what was devoted to God, in order to sacrifice them to the Lord your God at Gilgal."

22 But Samuel replied: "Does the Lord delight in burnt offerings and sacrifices as much as in obeying the Lord?

To obey is better than sacrifice, and to heed is better than the fat of rams.

To read that King Saul repeatedly lied to Samuel only made matters worst for him. Even Samuel pleaded with him and asked, "why lie?" An attributed saying to grandmothers, mothers, and big mommas around the world, "Tell the truth and shame the devil" was the piece of advice King Saul needed to take to heart. We must learn not to hide our sins from God. Like how we were first naked with God, that is how He wants us to return.

Not only was Saul lying, but he was also attempting to justify his wrong to Samuel. We have been bewitched when God sends people into our lives to rebuke us, and we try to convert them to side with us. We must not buck at rebuke but embrace correction and not miss the chance to receive much-needed prayer. The prayers of the righteous avails much (James 5:16). Saul was in front of Samuel, whose prayers were heard by the Almighty God. Saul missed his chance by lying and attempting to justify himself.

He wanted Samuel and, most importantly, God to accept and condone his actions. He was trying to tell God to accept wrong as right and right as wrong. This is why Prophet Samuel was open to telling him that obedience (doing the will of God) is better than sacrifice (works). In other words, "Who you say you are is not more important than what you do."

Do not run from the saving grace that we all so desperately need. It doesn't matter how many times we fall but how many times we stand. The Bible says we ought to forgive 77 times, and surely God is more merciful than any man (Matthew 18:21-22). Remain open and naked before God and confess your sins; He is faithful and just to forgive you for all unrighteousness.

THE BELOVED IS REJECTED: A GRAVE ERROR

1 Samuel 15:24-26

24 Then Saul said to Samuel, "I have sinned. I violated the Lord's command and your instructions. I was afraid of the men and so I gave in to them. 25 Now I beg you, forgive my sin and come back with me, so that I may worship the Lord."

26 But Samuel said to him, "I will not go back with you. You have rejected the word of the Lord, and the Lord has rejected you as king over Israel!"

There are always seasons in our lives when God allows us to repent and accept His grace. You will miss the mark if you don't discern God's timing or take grace for granted. King Saul is exhibit "A" for what happens when you miss the mark and close the door on grace. Because King Saul did not accept grace when it was given, he welcomed judgment upon his life.

Have you ever seen people that are in dire straits lacking food, clothes, and health, reject the help sent? When we turn away the help that God provides, it is to our own detriment. We cannot blame anyone but ourselves when our lives take a nasty turn for the worse.

The Bible says, "···for those who stand with me now, I will stand with you later (Matthew 10:33)." We do not want to be disowned by Jesus or God the Father because we have rejected Him. It is a huge insult for us to reject the Lord God, knowing He died for us when we were still sinners and hated Him (Romans 5:10). In Luke 9:26, the Bible also says, "Whoever is ashamed of me and my words, the Son of Man will be ashamed of them when He comes in His glory and in the glory of the Father and of the holy angels."

Is there a man, woman, person, place, or thing that can separate us from the Love of God (Romans 8:31-39)? Fear of rejection by our peers usually kindles this separation between God and us. Saul admitted to being more afraid of people and their opinions than fearing God.

His allegiance became to man instead of God. You see, Saul did not realize the people were attracted to the light that was in him, not him. People saw Saul as a victor, and so did the devil.

The devil loves nothing more than to see you,

and I fall from the place that God has appointed us. Saul did not realize that by siding with man, he sided with the devil and lost the presence of God. Once he lost the Presence of God, he also lost the people's approval.

When we maintain the Presence of God in our lives we are not supposed to compromise nor listen to the voice of other people. King Saul's biggest mistake was listening to the voices of men instead of obeying the voice of God. Saul fell from grace and shattered his purpose. According to this passage, God determined he was no longer fit to serve His purpose and He released him from being His servant.

While reflecting on Saul's biggest mistake, let's explore what happens when the Spirit of the Lord leaves.

1 Samuel 17:23-24

23 As he was talking with them, Goliath, the Philistine champion from Gath, stepped out from his lines and shouted his usual defiance, and David heard it.

24 Whenever the Israelites saw the man, they all fled from him in great fear.

When the spirit of the Lord leaves your life, grace and mercy follow. Saul was now left weak and humble, as he was before the presence of the Lord dwelled with him. When we lose our position and favor in the eyes of the Lord, two specific spirits linked to carnality rise up. The first is envy, and the second is jealousy.

When David came on the scene to fight Goliath, he exposed Saul's weaknesses to the nation. Why was the king, who had led many battles before and won, now fearful like the other people to fight Goliath? Where was his confidence, strength, and leadership? The confidence was in the presence of the Lord. Now that the voice of God was not in his ear to lead, Saul was on his own.

Even though Saul did not die instantly after his disobedience, like the prophet Iddo, his relationship with God was dead. Saul was a walking dead man, and it showed. He had no power, and those close to him knew the anointing had left him. Rage grew within Saul for the future king, David, because he constantly reminded him of his fall from grace.

<u>1 Samuel 18:8</u>

8 Saul was very angry; this refrain displeased him greatly. "They have credited David with tens of thousands," he thought, "but me with only thousands. What more can he get but the kingdom?"

When the young man, David, defeated Goliath, his renown increased among the people. Of course, prior to King David having the courage to face the giant, he, too, was anointed by Samuel with a kingly anointing. He was also the youngest, smallest, and most humble, as his chances of amassing wealth were slim. He had several older brothers entitled to his father's inheritance long before he would receive a thing. The Lord took this humble soul, the same as he took Saul, and began to lift him up. His journey started with fighting a lion and a bear before he challenged Goliath.

Saul knew all too well what was happening with young David better than anyone. When he saw David, he had to be reminded of his past, of his humble beginning. He started to hear of his fame. The words of the Almighty God were Saul's reality. Saul became envious of the song the people sang lifting David above his name.

The people said David killed ten thousand and Saul only a thousand. The people that Saul allowed to make him fall from grace are now the people who have turned their backs on him. The fame he grew all too comfortable with having had disappeared, and his envy was kindled against David.

1 Samuel 18:9

9 And from that time on Saul kept a close eye on David.

The spirit of envy festered in Saul, and jealousy was its twin. Saul, once the great leader favored by God, is now an outcast. Can you imagine being a big-time stockbroker who goes broke? How about a singer or star athlete who loses the praise and fame of the people who used to adore them?

How can they go from being rich to living a regular life or worse, become poor again? Nothing makes a person more envious and jealous than seeing another excel in their footsteps. When we choose not to walk in our gifts or obey the voice of the Lord, God will find another who is willing and able (Isaiah 6:8).

Don't allow envy and jealousy to take root because it will cause you to miss out on your destiny. We can get off track in life, but there can be a redemption story because the Lord is a redeemer of time (Joel 2:25). We should not envy each other's gifts, as we all have gifts to function in the body of Christ.

If you see another prospering, keep them in prayer. We don't know what it takes to maintain someone else's anointing. People can make assumptions and want what someone else has, but fight that urge. King David was not a perfect king, but he learned a lot following the rise and fall of Saul. No one elevates in God without learning some tough lessons. Keep your faith and eyes stayed on Jesus so that you may not fall into the traps. Carnality is not only brought on by the desire to appease other people but also to appease our own desires.

<u>1 Samuel 16:17-19</u>

17 So Saul said to his attendants, "Find someone who plays well and bring him to me."

18 One of the servants answered, "I have seen a son of Jesse of Bethlehem who knows how to play the lyre. He is a brave man and a warrior. He speaks well and is a fine-looking man. And the Lord is with him."

19 Then Saul sent messengers to Jesse and said, "Send me your son David, who is with the sheep."

When the joy of the Lord is not our strength, the works of the flesh take preeminence over your life. When Saul was seeking a replacement to sustain his joy, he sought out a remedy. Although music didn't solve his problems, it did soothe his emotions—and fears. He was frustrated to find that the same one he hated was the one to save him from himself.

It's funny how we try to make God our problem, only to find He is our solution. The best harp player in the country was the same one who gained more victories and was ordained to take his place as king, David. When we attempt to find solutions to fill the vacancy of losing the Presence of God in our lives, we learn that there is no replacement. Natural and narcotic highs are fleeting, and at the end, when the music stops and the high fades, the same anxieties are still there.

When David arrived to play for King Saul, the Presence of the Lord could be seen all over him; even Saul's children could see it. It's amazing how everyone has a hunger to be in the light, even if they do not live according to the light. You never hear about someone looking for a selfish, self-centered, unfriendly, unkind, unloving person, but the exact opposite! Saul's son, Jonathan, meets David, and they become good friends. Everything he had loved David.

When the Lord wants to show you something, there is no limit to what He will do to bring you in remembrance of Him. No matter what we do to try and escape God, there is nothing created that can fill the hole God leaves behind when He exits your life but Him. God had moved his anointing to David and gave him the favor Saul grew to love. The people admired David, and even Saul had to reward him with gifts after he killed Goliath. Saul saw God moving; He just wasn't moving with him any longer.

1 Samuel 17:8-10

8 Goliath stood and shouted to the ranks of Israel, "Why do you come out and line up for battle? Am I not a Philistine, and are you not the servants of Saul? Choose a man and have him come down to me.

9 If he is able to fight and kill me, we will become your subjects; but if I overcome him and kill him, you will become our subjects and serve us."

10 Then the Philistine said, "This day I defy the armies of Israel! Give me a man and let us fight each other."

Another shift that takes place in our lives is when the Presence of God departs, fear takes its rightful place, replacing our trust and love with fear. Love casts out fear (1 John 4:18), and God is Love (1 John 4:17). Have you ever noticed that when people are fearful, they will give away everything to be secure?

Even if the security is false, the flesh can trick us into believing that giving up something real is worth something intangible. Saul gave his daughter away to anyone who would defeat Goliath. When you hand everything over for security, you find that you lose everything.

Only the Lord can save, protect, and keep us no matter the circumstance. There is a large space in all of our lives that can only be filled with God's Presence, also known as His Spirit. If that place is empty, the devil and demons come to try and keep you distracted, chasing other things so you don't realize it. The help of the Lord keeps the demons away. Resist the devil, and he will flee (James 4:7). Well, if you have not submitted yourself to God, by what authority can you send the demons fleeing?

When the twelve disciples were working and carrying out ministry, they came across a strange spirit, a demon that told them, "Paul and Jesus I know, but who are you (Acts 19:15)?" You see, your spirit bears witness to who and what you are. If you have the Spirit of the Lord, your actions will bear fruit to validate your claims (Matthew 7:16). Saul's fear was exposed in this passage, and he no longer believed the Lord would deliver his enemies into his hands.

Saul was scared that if he went into battle, he would die, and rightfully so. When God's Presence left, he had to start relying on people to deliver him. The very thing he loved, he lost. He loved to be adored and celebrated. Now, he is a has-been with a kingdom already discontent with his rule.

He had many sleepless nights because he was worried about losing his kingdom to David. I am sure he thought David would attack him for the throne, but that wasn't how he operated. If the two of them went to war, he wasn't sure if the people would side with him or David.

1 Samuel 17:33

33 Saul replied, "You are not able to go out against this Philistine and fight him; you are only a young man, and he has been a warrior from his youth."

Saul not only lost all faith in God but also lost his vision to see into the spirit. He believed the Philistine would devour David because he was focused and looking on the flesh instead of peering into the spirit. The spiritual realm he could not peer into any longer because the Presence and the Spirit of the Lord had left him. Without the Spirit of God, we cannot see the world as it truly is but as it looks to the naked eye.

This is life without faith; you have to live by sight because you cannot see to walk by the Spirit. When David talked about defeating Goliath, Saul, I am sure, thought he went mad. The Bible says, "God uses the foolish things in order to shame those that think they are wise (1 Corinthians 1:27)." Yes, God can use a willing vessel that doesn't stand tall, has nothing but a rock, slingshot, and Faith. Faith in God makes you mighty and able to tear down any stronghold.

Saul forgot about the battles he won that were not won because of his strategy and ideas but because of the Presence of God. It is very easy to take your health for granted, people for granted, and even God for granted. When your body is up and working as it should, many of us hardly think about the food we eat. The moment that our body starts to break down and sickness creeps in, we then look to receive healing and perhaps seek out change.

If we are not careful, we can misuse God's Presence and be so comfortable with knowing He is there that we forget to revere His Presence. The Lord God is holy, and we must acknowledge Him like a Holy King and not even remotely similar to a man. If we treat the Lord like we treat our bodies or like we treat people, we can take Him for granted and not notice when He left our lives.

Saul thought his strength was in himself, his title, his kingdom, and the things the Lord made him a steward over but not an owner of. We are all stewards in this life over what we have because none of us can take a thing with us when we die. Don't sell your soul short; the kingdom is awaiting those who seek His Kingdom first (Matthew 6:33).

THE AFTERMATH: WHEN GOD'S PRESENCE LEAVES

1 Samuel 18:10-11

10 The next day an evil spirit from God came forcefully on Saul. He was prophesying in his house, while David was playing the lyre, as he usually did. Saul had a spear in his hand

11 and he hurled it, saying to himself, "I'll pin David to the wall." But David eluded him twice.

When you seek the Kingdom of God and His righteousness, be prepared for the Lord to add everything you need and desire. The Lord does this not out of obligation but because He cares for you (1 Peter 5:7). Verse 10 requires a closer look.

We read that God sent an evil spirit. The Bible said that God would give us the desires of our hearts (Psalm 37:4).

If we delight in the Lord, He will give us our desire for more of Him, good and lovely things. If we don't delight in the Lord, what do you think you should receive? As a man thinks, so is he. If you think about bad, deadly, and cursed things, those things will manifest, which is why the Bible instructs us to think about things that are good and lovely. If you do not serve the Lord, you are under the cloud of serving the prince of the air, the devil's territory. Devil worshippers are not only the people wearing creepy clothes, upside down crosses, etc, but those who have separated themselves from Yah.

Verse ten says God sent an evil spirit to Saul. Wow! I had to read that a few times because it is so sad to know that God's face is set against you. Who can fight God? I am sure his life was miserable, and to be possessed by an evil spirit should have been the lowest position he could go in life.

One sin that no one can save you from is blaspheming against the Holy Spirit (Mark 3:28-30). Esaw and Cain both made choices that too displeased the Lord; Cain was rejected and never was engrafted back in. Yet, David would murder a man and receive mercy.

We cannot take any actions to restore what He says is forever broken. If you have made mistakes, and it is not too late to repent and plead for mercy, do so. Let your heart not be hardened, filled with pride, or hold a haughty spirit. These attitudes and spirits do not please the Lord but turn Him away from you. Saul forgot his first love, and his works displeased the Lord. Giving him way to his evil desires was his heart's desire.

If his heart desired to please the Lord, he would have gotten mercy like Paul, King David, and all those who desired the Lord. Realizing our depraved state of being is the first step to repentance and desiring the Lord. Never outgrow repentance, and mercy will be available. Saul not only lost his mind, but he had an evil mind.

1 Samuel 18:12-17

12 Saul was afraid of David, because the Lord was with David but had departed from Saul.

13 So he sent David away from him and gave him command over a thousand men, and David led the troops in their campaigns.

14 In everything he did he had great success, because the Lord was with him.

15 When Saul saw how successful he was, he was afraid of him.

16 But all Israel and Judah loved David, because he led them in their campaigns.

17 Saul said to David, "Here is my older daughter Merab. I will give her to you in marriage; only serve me bravely and fight the battles of the Lord." For Saul said to himself, "I will not raise a hand against him. Let the Philistines do that!"

Instead of turning from his evil mindset, Saul

gave more into it. His mind was not affixed to doing the will of God but evil. He plotted against God's chosen and attempted to trick him because he didn't like him. What bothered Saul so much about David, aside from him being his replacement? I would surmise it was that David was becoming everything Saul wanted, and he had the grace to make the call look easy.

The Lord used David to show Saul the mistake he made in denouncing God for things, people, and fame. Saul lost his fame with the people to David, and he didn't stop at any cost to redeem his power. He offered his daughter and requested that David fight a battle that he thought he would lose. He forgot not to trouble the Lord's anointed (Psalm 105:15).

David was called by God, and he followed the Lord's instructions. When we are in step with God's commands, nothing can harm us. Saul, with all his power and presumed wisdom, thought he could trap David, and all he did was stir up more fear within himself.

Saul feared David because he saw the hand of God on his life. When the Lord's hand is on your life, no one can remove it. Saul was willing to give his daughter to the Lord but not himself. How can you compete when everything around you shouts the plan of God?

1 Samuel 19:4-5

4 Jonathan spoke well of David to Saul his father and said to him, "Let not the king do wrong to his servant David; he has not wronged you, and what he has done has benefited you greatly.

5 He took his life in his hands when he killed the Philistine. The Lord won a great victory for all Israel, and you saw it and were glad. Why then would you do wrong to an innocent man like David by killing him for no reason?"

His son, Jonathan, loved David. So even those who were presumed to be in Saul's corner were being used by the Lord. His daughter was David's wife, and his son was David's best friend. The kingdom, too, belonged to the Lord, and that was being given to David.

Saul's evil mind did not set him free but bound him in fear. When we don't repent, we easily fall into living out of fear. Fear begets an evil mindset and attempts to destroy anything good.

David respected Saul, and never attempted to kill him—even when he could have. He served Saul wholeheartedly and the Lord admired him for his perfect trust in the Lord. David respected the office of the king and showed himself worthy of the throne.

It is tempting to over through a person's office when you see their flaws. Resist the urge because you will find favor with the Lord. Respect authority and pray for them instead.

1 Samuel 22:17-19

17 Then the king ordered the guards at his side: "Turn and kill the priests of the Lord, because they too have sided with David. They knew he was fleeing, yet they did not tell me."

But the king's officials were unwilling to raise a hand to strike the priests of the Lord.

18 The king then ordered Doeg, "You turn and strike down the priests." So Doeg the Edomite turned and struck them down. That day he killed eighty-five men who wore the linen ephod. 19 He also put to the sword Nob, the town of the priests, with its men and women, its children and infants, and its cattle, donkeys and sheep.

Saul failed to kill David and took his disappointment and hatred out on innocent people who, too, loved and served God. People ripped with fear, hatred, rejection, and pride kill innocent people. A similar situation in our world is when a person shoots up a school, movie theater, church, and such places to wage war on innocent bystanders.

Some have even asked their victims if they believed in Jesus, and when they said "yes," they shot them at point-blank range. Millions of martyrs died believing in the Lord. Truly, God didn't let any of them down by calling them home. To be apart from the earth—for believers, is to be present with God.

We must not forget that it is the Lord who enacts revenge, not us (Romans 12:19). When people are guilty of heinous crimes like these, we must not engulf ourselves with hatred, fear, or vengeance. If we allow these emotions—spirits—to grab ahold of us, we lose the battle. We must stand strong in God and not reject His teachings. He tells us to put our trust in Him.

Perfect trust requires us to believe and pray the hand of God to vindicate His people. Saul confirmed his death by his horrendous sins; some sins are unto death (1 John 5:1-17). His pride sent him down a rabbit hole of destruction, and he never set his heart on repenting. When he did ask to be forgiven, he was ingenious with Samuel and wanted him to do all the praying for him.

He didn't cry out to Yah like Hezikiah after his sin, which should have led to his death. He was given fifteen more years because he found favor with the Lord again. Saul didn't have a repentant heart but sought prayer only because he got caught.

1 Samuel 28:5-6

5 When Saul saw the Philistine army, he was afraid; terror filled his heart. **6** He inquired of the Lord, but the Lord did not answer him by dreams or Urim or prophets.

Saul was comfortable turning his back on the Lord when he thought he had a good handle on life. This false power quickly disappeared. With the progression of the Philistines and the imminent threat of invasion, he realized he was a man and no match for an army. He needed the Lord. He didn't want the Lord because he loved God but because he wanted God's glory to show up again.

In life, we can deceive ourselves to believe we pursue God because we love him. Saul was scared and desperate to find comfort. He was willing now to disguise his pride because fear was stronger than pride. When he called on the name of the

Lord to rescue him, the Lord turned a deaf ear to Saul. We cannot tempt, nor will God be mocked (Galatians 6:7).

We cannot trick God into saving us or deceive Him. God knows the heart of every man, and He looks upon the heart. The Bible says the heart is wicked, and only God knows it (Jeremiah 17:10).

God knows what is in your heart. When you say you repented, if you are not genuine, the Lord knows it. God turned a deaf ear to Saul because his heart was far from Him. We know that Saul also wasn't genuine because when God denied him, he consulted familiar spirits.

1 Samuel 28:7-11

7 Saul then said to his attendants, "Find me a woman who is a medium, so I may go and inquire of her."

"There is one in Endor," they said.

8 So Saul disguised himself, putting on other clothes, and at night he and two men went to the woman. "Consult a spirit for me," he said, "and bring up for me the one I name."

9 But the woman said to him, "Surely you know what Saul has done. He has cut off the mediums and spiritists from the land. Why have you set a trap for my life to bring about my death?"

10 Saul swore to her by the Lord, "As surely as the Lord lives, you will not be punished for this."

11 Then the woman asked, "Whom shall I bring

up for you?"

"Bring up Samuel," he said.

Saul gave in to seducing spirits, and because the Lord rejected his prayers, he turned to divination. Fear made him reach his lowest of lows. An evil spirit possessed him, but now he is going to those same spirits for answers. Wow! Saul was losing more of his mind as he lived on. He didn't get the rest he so desperately wanted except during the playing of music. He went to a psychic to help him discern the future because the unknown eluded and scared him. He allowed fear to scare him to death. Spiritually, he was dead, and his flesh was not too far behind.

If your life is in God's hands, you need not worry if you don't hear His Voice all the time. Have the confidence of the believer to know that the Lord is working all things to your good. When the Lord removes His hand, desperation may tempt you to seek the devil for help. This, too, only increases the wedge between you and God.

This verse also points to Saul's true heart. His spirit was not becoming like the Savior but a wandering spirit. In his later years, Saul had a spirit more like a devil worshipper than a child of God. Don't lose faith in God because there is no greater name or presence than His glory. Saul sought out a woman of divination and asked her to resurrect a man of God.

He woke Samuel from his rest to ask him to plead to God on his behalf; that, too, failed. Samuel was the one who originally bestowed the opportunity for him to repent. When Saul thought he was ready to repent, God was not interested in listening. The time had passed for him. Yes, it is possible to miss your chance at redemption.

A Lesson For us All

This book was written to highlight the issues that Saul faced and how we, too, face similar problems today. Saul went from rags to riches, the perfect example of the American dream.

He needed help during his time of need, and so did the nation. God can use anyone and everyone for a great cause. We don't all have to be kings, but we are all royalty when we are part of His kingdom.

We are a royal priesthood and a peculiar people (1 Peter 2:9). Saul started off with the right heart, but his heart turned from God. The Bible tells us to guard our hearts (Proverbs 4:23). We are to guard our hearts because if we leave the door open, anything or anyone can walk in. The devil roams around like a hungry lion, seeing who he can devour (1 Peter 5:8). Fiery darts from the enemy are flying to strike us (Ephesians 6:16).

We must follow the Lord's Prayer and remember why it is important. He tells us to forgive others like how He forgives us. Forgiveness is a process between the receiver and the giver. If one does not participate, forgiveness can be a challenge.

It is impossible to please God and make it into heaven with unforgiveness in your heart–we must forgive (Isaiah 59:1-2). Forgiveness is done to please God, and it frees us from bondage. By offering and receiving forgiveness, we help each other and cast off heavy weights.

We are to live as examples so that the world can see and experience God here on earth. It was never Yah's intent for men to rule over men as kings. God was to be king and ruler over all. Humility is a virtue that should not be cast aside. Christ even embodied humility while walking this earth, and we should, too.

Saul grieved the Holy Spirit with his actions, reaction to his sin, and continued steps to please his own agenda. God wants us to remember our first love. He desires that we always put His thoughts, desires, and plans as our priority. It is only what God thinks and says that should dictate our life decisions. Saul started his journey with God by obeying His Word, principles, and Voice.

He grew to believe that perhaps he deserved the position, the title, the office of king. He had fought battles and won. He fit the physical physique of a king, and the people loved him. He forgot, however, that the Lord came and built him up. He came from the smallest tribe. He was not born of promise, but God said something different and called him blessed.

God chose Saul, and Saul returned the favor by disowning Him. He believed in the hype and disobeyed God. He exchanged God's thoughts for the thoughts of others. He put man before God.

Saul's end was wallowing in fear. Fear ate him from the inside out, and every move he made was out of terror. The power he thought he had faded. The fame he had with the people was drowned out by David killing tens of thousands. The people stopped singing his praises and switched to those of David. His children sided with the future king, and the prophet who called him, Samuel, also embraced David.

Saul had lost everything—his relationship with God, his office, the kingdom, and his life—when he separated from God. Our lives will be the same, going in a downward cycle that will end with us having nothing. No peace, no hope, and fear will rest in our hearts and minds.

Don't allow fear, doubt, and pride to separate you from God's love. If sin or unforgiveness barricades your prayers from reaching heaven, renounce your sin, praying in spirit and truth. Forgive those who hurt and trespassed against you. The only way to move God is to follow His way. To please God and receive salvation, we must pray in spirit and truth (John 4:24).

About the Author

"God blesses those who work for peace, for they will be called the children of God." Matthew 5:9

Krystal Lee is proud to have authored this book and accompanying course to better the lives of readers. She has a heart to help people in their deepest times of need. She writes because she believes there is power in sharing stories and life accounts, that others can benefit and learn from. Sharing is caring, so she shares stories, ideas, and resources to better the lives of her readers.

In addition, Dr. Lee has authored over 20 books across seven or more genres (adult, children, youth fiction, self-help, spiritual growth, novels, and more), in addition to ghostwriting and editing more than 15 published works. She has launched coaching programs, web courses, and helped in the formulation of many startup companies. Her specialty lies in aiding coaches, creatives, and service-based companies in defining their message, brand, unique selling point, client avatar, and generating a sales cycle and structure for her clients.

Empowering individuals is at the core of her work, and she is driven by her passion to continue writing. In addition to being an author, Krystal Lee is a business owner of multiple companies, a consultant, an ordained chaplain, and a speaker.

For more information about Dr. Krystal Lee or to engage with her further, please scan the provided QR code. To engage with the Coaching series and Monthly Meet up Group for Embrace Your Crown First Sundays at 4pm, please use the QR code or visit KLEembrace.com

Shop Books from AuthorKLee.com

Explore over seven different book genres, and find something suitable for every member of the family.

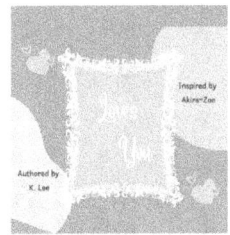

Scan to Shop All Titles by K. Lee

It's time to start and finish **YOUR Story**!

KLE Publishing specializes in helping people become authors. In as little as 15 to 90 days, we can help you develop your book and publish to 39,000 outlets!

Ghostwrite, Edit, Format, Publish
We can help from **Start to Finish.**

Scan and fill out the short form to learn more and connect with us.

KLEPub.com Authors

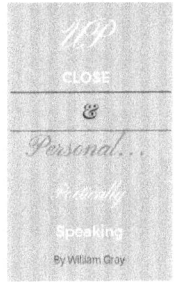

www.ingramcontent.com/pod-product-compliance
Lightning Source LLC
Chambersburg PA
CBHW052119110526
44592CB00013B/1679